ANGRY

First published 1990
by Cherrytree Press Ltd
Windsor Bridge Road
Bath, Avon BA2 3AX England

First published in the United States 1991
by Raintree Publishers, A Division of Steck-Vaughn Company

Library of Congress Number: 90-46540

Library of Congress Cataloging-in-Publication Data

Amos, Janine.
   Feelings/by Janine Amos; illustrated by Gwen Green.
   Cover title.
   Contents: [1] Afraid—[2] Angry—[3] Hurt—[4] Jealous—[5] Lonely—[6] Sad.
   1. Emotions—Case studies—Juvenile literature. [1. Emotions.] I. Green, Gwen, ill. II. Title.
BF561.A515   1991
152.4—dc20   90-46540
                                                                               CIP
                                                                               AC

ISBN 0-8172-3776-3   hardcover library binding

ISBN 0-8114-6909-3   softcover binding

Other hardcover ISBNs: Afraid   0-8172-3775-5   Lonely   0-8172-3779-8
                          Hurt   0-8172-3777-1   Sad   0-8172-3780-1
                          Jealous   0-8172-3778-X

   4 5 6 7 8 9   95 94 93 92

ANGRY

By Janine Amos
Illustrated by Gwen Green

RSVP
RAINTREE
STECK-VAUGHN
PUBLISHERS
The Steck-Vaughn Company

Austin, Texas

JOSH'S STORY

Josh put the last piece of his model in place. Making a moon buggy out of the little plastic building blocks had taken a long time. He'd had to use a few wheels and other pieces from different toys. But it was the best thing he'd ever made.

"Look at my moon buggy!" said Josh. Very slowly he carried the model from his room toward the kitchen. His little brother Tim came to look.

"It's great!" said Tim. He touched it carefully and turned one of the wheels. "Can I play with it while you're at Little League?"

"No!" Josh said. "No one can touch it!"

"Josh, don't be selfish," called their mom from the other room. "Let Tim play with it."

Josh groaned and said, "Promise you won't drop it!"

Tim promised.

Josh's team lost the game. When he got home, he was tired. He changed out of his uniform and went into the kitchen for a can of pop. Tim was there, playing with his friend Justin. They were playing with the building blocks.

Josh looked at the table. His moon buggy was gone.

"Where's my model?" he asked. But the boys were busy and didn't hear him. Josh went over to Tim.

"Where's my moon buggy?" he said again, in a loud voice.

"We wanted to make a windmill," Tim said.

"You took my moon buggy apart!" shouted Josh.

How do you think Josh feels right now?

Josh picked up the windmill and threw it on the floor.
Then he punched Tim. Tim fell down and started to cry.
"I hate you!" shouted Josh. He hit his brother again.

When their mom heard the noise, she rushed in and told
them to stop fighting. But Josh was too angry and upset to
hear. His mom had to pull him away from Tim.

"Calm down," Josh's mom said.

"I won't!" Josh yelled. "He ruined my model!"

"Upstairs!" his mom ordered. "Right now!"

Josh ran up to his bedroom and slammed the door. He was shaking all over. He felt as if he was about to explode. He fell on the bed and started to cry with loud sobs. He was frightened.

Why do you think Josh is frightened?

Josh's mom came in and sat down next to him.

"Go away," Josh sobbed. "You're on Tim's side."

"No, I'm not," his mom said quietly.

At last Josh stopped shaking and crying. But his throat hurt, and he was very tired.

"Do you feel better now?" his mom asked. Josh nodded.

"Your model was really great, Josh," she said. "No wonder you were so angry when Tim took it apart."

"I hit him so hard I almost killed him," Josh whispered.

"No, you didn't," his mom said. "Maybe for a minute you felt like you wanted to, but Tim's okay."

"I don't like getting that mad," said Josh. "It's scary."

"Yes," said his mom, "but it's all right to feel angry. It isn't all right to hit someone, though. Instead, you could have told Tim how upset you were. You could have asked him to help you make another moon buggy."

Later Josh built a new moon buggy. He worked on it by himself. But when it was finished he showed it to Tim.

"I'm sorry I took your other model apart," Tim said. "It was neat. You were really mad, weren't you?"

"Yes," said Josh. "I was, but just for a while."

Tim looked at the new model.

"This one's better than the first one," he said.

How did Josh's mom help when Josh was feeling angry?

Feeling like Josh

Have you ever felt angry, the way Josh did? Have you ever been so mad that you thought you might hurt someone? If you have, you know how upsetting it can be to feel anger so strongly. You might yell and shake. You might feel that anger has taken over your whole body. You might feel out of control.

Good reasons

Often there are good reasons to be angry. Someone may break something that belongs to you, or destroy something you made, or lose something of yours. It's good to let someone know how angry you feel. But losing control of yourself won't help. And it may frighten you and make you feel even worse afterwards.

Anger isn't bad

It isn't wrong to feel angry. Everyone gets mad and upset sometimes. But there are many ways of showing anger. Sometimes, like Josh, your angry feelings may come out too strongly. Learning to show your feelings without getting too upset can be difficult. If you find it hard, ask someone else for help. Tell a grown-up, like a parent or teacher, how you feel.

Think about it

Read the stories in this book. Think about the people in the stories. Do you sometimes feel the way they do? Next time you feel angry, ask yourself some questions: What am I angry about? What have I done when I was angry before? What is the best thing to do now? Who can I talk to about it?

GINA'S STORY

It was time for the race. Gina waited at the starting line. She waved to her father and brother Mike. Then she looked at the other girls waiting to run. Most of them seemed nervous. Only Anne was smiling. Anne was a good runner, but she wasn't as fast as Gina.

"Get ready!" called a voice. A whistle blew, and they were off. Gina got a good head start. She felt the soft grass under her shoes. She heard the crowd cheering. And she knew she could win.

Very soon Gina could see the faces of the people at the finish line. She knew she was ahead of all the other girls. But then she tripped. She wobbled, but she didn't stop running. Her heart was beating hard. Suddenly Anne raced past her and crossed the finish line!

Gina couldn't believe it! It had all happened so fast. People were crowding around.

"Way to go, Anne! Good race!" they said. "Too bad, Gina. Better luck next time." Gina turned away.

Gina's father and brother were waiting for her. She ran over to them.

"We can start the picnic now," said Mike. But Gina wouldn't eat anything.

"You must be thirsty," her father said. He offered her some lemonade. Gina threw the cup down. Then she walked away, stamping her feet in the grass.

How does Gina feel right now? How do you think her father feels?

Gina watched her friends and their families. Most of them were having picnics in the grass. Everyone seemed to be having a good time. But Gina wasn't.

After a while her father came and sat next to her.

"Are you still upset?" he asked. Gina nodded.

"Well, maybe it's time to stop," her father said. "You missed the picnic, and now you're spoiling the afternoon for yourself and everyone else."

"I can't help it," said Gina.

"You can try," said her father. He gave her a hug.

"I hate losing," Gina said.

"So do I," her father said. "It's hard to lose, and being a good loser is even harder."

Do you think Gina's father is right? Are you a good loser?

Feeling like Gina

Gina didn't win the race, and it made her angry. She was upset with herself. If you are feeling like Gina, it may help to remember that everyone loses sometimes; nobody wins all the time. You can only do your best. Everyone has to learn how to be a good loser sometimes.

Let the anger go

If you feel like Gina, it may help to talk about it. Keeping your feelings inside and thinking about how angry you are won't help. It didn't make Gina feel better and made her miss the picnic fun. So try to let go of your anger. Take a deep breath, then let it out slowly. Do it again. You will feel calmer.

PAUL'S STORY

Paul and his mother were at the train station. They were going to visit Paul's Aunt Kate. Paul had never been on a real train before.

"We'll have lunch on the train," said his mother. "And you can sit next to the window if you want to."

"Sure!" said Paul. He was excited.

The station was very busy. Paul jumped as a man whizzed past, pushing a cart.

"Stay close to me, Paul," his mother said. "Our train leaves from over there." She pointed across the station. She picked up their suitcase and started walking quickly down some steps. Paul ran along behind. But at that moment a crowd of people came toward them.

"Wait, Mom!" Paul shouted. Now all he could see were arms, legs, and other people's suitcases. He couldn't see his mother anywhere.

Paul squeezed through the crowd. A big man pushed him. "Get out of my way, kid," said the man, puffing. "I'm late."

"I'm lost," thought Paul. He felt scared.

Paul stopped at the bottom of the steps. He didn't know what to do. He decided to wait right there.

It seemed like he waited for a long time. He started to worry.

"I bet we missed the train," he thought.

Then Paul heard someone calling his name. His mother ran toward him. But she didn't look happy.

"I told you to stay close to me!" she shouted. "Don't you dare get lost again!"

Paul's eyes filled with tears, and his face got red.

His mother grabbed his arm and said, "Come on, or we'll miss the train."

"I don't want to!" Paul pulled away. "Let me go!"

How do you think Paul's mother feels?
How would you feel now if you were Paul?

Paul lost his temper.

"It's your fault!" he yelled at his mother. "You went too fast!" He stamped his feet. He threw his new jacket on the ground. "You lost *me!*" He was so angry that he was shaking. People stopped to stare at him. He felt so awful he started to cry.

Just then they heard a voice on the loudspeaker.

"Listen," Paul's mother said. "That's our train!"

She grabbed his hand, and they both ran as fast as they could. Together they ran up some more stairs. A conductor was standing on the train steps. He said the train was ready to go and they were just in time.

By the time they sat down, Paul had stopped feeling so angry. He was just very tired.

"Shall we have some lunch?" his mother asked.

Paul didn't answer. He stared out the window.

"Hey, come on," his mother said. "Let's be friends again."

"I'm sorry I yelled at you," said Paul's mother. "It wasn't your fault. I shouldn't have blamed you."

"I'm sorry I yelled back," Paul said. "I was scared because I was lost."

"I was scared too," she told him. "That's why I shouted at you."

"What do you mean?" Paul asked. "I don't understand why you yelled at me when you *found* me!"

His mother laughed. "I don't understand either!" she said.

How did Paul and his mother make up and become friends again? Is it easy for you to say you're sorry?

Feeling like Paul

Paul's mother was frightened and worried. And she was still upset when she found him. That's why she shouted. But Paul didn't get lost on purpose. He was worried too. When his mother yelled at him, he got angry. He thought she was being unfair, so he yelled back at her. But that didn't do any good. It just made both of them more upset. They almost missed the train.

Anger doesn't last

Sometimes angry feelings seem to last forever. And that can be scary. It helps to remember that very angry feelings don't last a long time. And you can make up and be friends again, no matter how angry you've been.

Saying you're sorry

Arguing with friends and people you love can be upsetting. Saying you're sorry is a good way to end an argument. It shows that you're over being angry and that you're ready to be friends again. Talking about your feelings afterward, the way Paul and his mother did, will make both of you feel better.

Think about it

Think about the stories in this book. Josh, Gina, and Paul each got angry for a different reason. Josh was angry because someone ruined something he made. Gina was angry with herself because she lost a race. Paul was angry because his mother yelled at him for something that wasn't his fault. They all showed their anger in different ways, but they didn't feel any better until they let go of the angry feelings. Talking about those feelings helped them. If you feel angry and upset, try talking about the problem with someone you trust. Talking about your anger will help you, just as it helped Josh, Gina, and Paul.

If you are feeling frightened or unhappy, don't keep it to yourself. Talk to an adult you can trust:

- one of your parents or other relatives
- a friend's parent or other relative
- a teacher
- the principal
- someone else at school
- a neighbor
- someone at a church, temple, or synagogue

You can also find someone to talk to about a problem by calling places called "hotlines." One hotline is **Child Help,** which you can call from anywhere in the United States. Just call

1-800-422-4453

from any telephone. You don't need money to call.

Or look in the phone book to find another phone number of people who can help. Try

- Children and Family Service
- Family Service

Remember you can always call the Operator in any emergency. Just dial 0 or press the button that says 0 on the telephone.